FAMILYLIFE™

50 nights of family fun!

Turn off the Tube & Turn up the Laughs

by Mark Whitlock

Fifty Nights of Family Fun:
Turn off the Tube and Turn up the Laughs

Author:	Mark Whitlock
Project Coordinator:	Shannon McGill
Graphic Designer:	Fran Wadkins
Editor:	Amy Bradford
Additional Editing:	Susan Matthews
	Anne Wooten
	Shannon McGill

FAMILYLIFE™
Bringing Timeless Principles Home

Dennis Rainey, President
5800 Ranch Drive
Little Rock, Arkansas 72223
(501) 223-8663
1-800-FL-TODAY
www.familylife.com
A division of Campus Crusade for Christ

The Hurried Life
Take a Step Toward Slowing Down—Fast From TV
by Dennis Rainey

I believe we have highly undervalued the importance of Sabbath rests. How badly do you need a Sabbath rest in your life? Maybe you're thinking, *Where can I find time to rest? I don't even have time to finish the things already on my to-do list. I'm stretched to the max!* Something has to give in your schedule—something must be set aside.

I want to challenge you to take one small step towards slowing down your life: set aside one element of the schedule you can control—the television. Spend one month—thirty-one days—"fasting" from television.

I know this won't be easy. TV has become a permanent addition to our culture, and perhaps to your home. Did you know that the average American watches more than four hours of television a day?[1] August is a great month to turn off the tube—the networks are only showing re-runs, basketball season is over, football hasn't started yet, and the baseball playoffs are still months away.

Fasting from TV will limit isolation in your family. Your fast will give you time to do all those little things you've been putting off. It will cause you to take a close look at the amount of time your family sits in front of the TV and to think of better ways to use that time.

Our family has done this, and I encourage you to do the same. You'll be amazed at the amount of time you will regain at home. Pray with me for God to control our schedules, lighten our loads, and help us to more deeply enjoy our families.

Go for it! I know you can do it!

Dennis Rainey

Dennis Rainey

[1] From www.tv-turnoff.org/factsheets.htm "Facts and Figures About or TV Habit." Retrieved on June 3, 2002

Table of Contents

There's a Stranger in Our House

by Mark Whitlock

Every spring, the weather in Arkansas is unpredictable. The last time the wind and rain knocked our power out, I discovered our family in the den ... staring with blank eyes at a mysterious stranger. Our darkened television. Unfortunately, I sat down on the couch and joined them.

What would you do if the power went out in your home? If your family is like mine, you need to break out of the TV rut. FamilyLife's challenge to turn off the TV off is a big one. (Read Dennis Rainey's challenge on page 3.) To be successful, your family will need boredom busters!

While we love watching videos and good television programs in our home, we also love to have fun. From family devotions on Monday nights to spontaneous wrestling matches with the kids, my wife and I have tried to keep our home full of laughter and grounded in God's Word.

Here are some of our favorite ideas. We've tried to keep them simple, easy-to-follow, and somewhat wacky. Feel free to improvise, or even improve them! As you try these ideas, do us a favor: don't stress out about your TV fast. Your screen might pop on. You might skip a night. Don't worry about it. You're making an intentional effort to connect with your family. Remember that.

Here are 50 boredom busters.

Pick 31 you like from these 10 categories:

- Spiritual Calisthenics

   Exercises for the growing theological athlete

- Scripture Journeys

  Short jaunts through God's valley of visions

- Focus on Others

  Ways to "do unto others ..."

- Home Improvement

  Tim Taylor has nothing on these projects.

- You've Got Rhythm

  The Bible calls music a joyful noise for a reason.

- Let the Games Begin

  Will you earn a medal of gold, silver, or tinfoil?

- Excursions

  Trips in your own backyard

- Creative Classics

  Play with colors, shapes, and textures—
  smocks optional.

- Literature Library

  Get your library cards ready.

- Family Ties

  Long distance family reunions

Spiritual Calisthenics

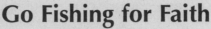

Go Fishing for Faith

Ask yourself a question: How do you know there are fish below the surface of the ocean? Faith. Books and pictures tell you they exist. Your experience has provided evidence. The other fishermen on the water give testimony. Faith.

Hebrews 11:1 says, "Now faith is the assurance of things hoped for, the conviction of things not seen" (NASB). Tonight, help your children better understand this abstract concept by creating a fishing hole in your home.

Go to the store and buy some small packaged snacks or candies. These will become your fish. Then, hang a blanket vertically in such a way that your children can't look over it or see behind it. Let each child fashion a fishing pole out of a stick, some yarn, and a spring-loaded clothespin for a hook.

Have your children take turns casting their lines over the blanket. Sometimes, clip a snack on the hook—sometimes, don't. After each of your children makes at least one "catch," tell each one that he will get one more chance to cast, and that each will receive another goody.

After every child has had a turn, gather in a circle and explain, "The last time you went fishing, you knew that you were going to get a snack, right? In the same way, God tells us that He is in heaven and that He loves you and cares for you. Just like you believed me, you can believe God. It's called faith."

Close in prayer, asking God to give each of you greater faith.

"What If...?"

Some lessons are only learned by experience. Tonight, use simple role playing techniques to teach a lesson. We've provided a role playing situation in this book (see below) or you can make up your own.[2]

How Good Is Your Word?
by Greg Johnson

It's Sunday afternoon and you just arrived home from church. The weather doesn't look too promising and there's not much on the tube. Dad comes to the rescue for a while by getting out the Scrabble game and keeping it lively. That kills an hour and a half. But you know you can't let him entertain you all day.

Time for Plan B. You go to your room, grab a book and start reading. After about half an hour, your eyes get heavy and you fall fast asleep ... for an hour! Mom wakes you up with an offer for an afternoon snack. Hey, that's a no-brainer.

It's still only late afternoon. After pestering your little brother for a while, you head down the street to see what a friend is doing. Not home. So you decide to walk down to the school playground to see if there's anything happening down there. Surprisingly, it's deserted. The clouds must have kept everyone away.

By the time you walk in the door back at home you're

---

[2] If you have fun with this one, try others. FamilyLife offers 31 different role playing situations on an audiocassette called "What If...?"

going crazy with boredom. But of course, Mom has a great suggestion: "A few chores will help pass the time."

Good ol' Mom! Always one to come to the rescue.

After you're done sweeping and raking the yard and vacuuming the car, it's dinnertime. That's when you hear the best news of the day.

"You know how you all have been wanting to see that movie at the two-dollar theater?" Dad says.

Everyone's eyes light up.

"Well, it's been kind of a boring day. Why don't we jump in the car and try to catch the early evening show?" he says.

Fantabulous!

While Dad finishes up the dishes and you're getting ready, the phone rings. Mom says it's for you, but to make it quick.

"Are you still coming over tonight?" asks the voice on the other end.

"Coming over? Tonight? What do you mean?" you say in a surprised tone.

"Don't you remember you told me as we were leaving school Friday that you'd come over Sunday night and help me with our science homework? Well, I'm ready for some help, and my mom said she'd pick you up."

"Oh, yeah. Now I remember. Well...

Questions to Think About
- What do you think you would say? Why?
- Have you ever had to choose between keeping your word and doing something you really wanted to do? What did you do?
- How important is it to you that other people keep their word with you?
- What do you see as a potential solution to this situation?
- Mom and Dad: What would you recommend your child do?

What Does God Have to Say?

The Lord detests lying lips, but he delights in men who are truthful.

Proverbs 12:22

Who is going to harm you if you are eager to do good?
1 Peter 3:13

Missions Journey Without a Passport

Biographies written by missionaries can be some of the richest sources of spiritual challenge. Over several nights, take turns reading one aloud as a family. Read one chapter each night from a book like *Through Gates of Splendor* by Elisabeth Elliot Gren or *God's Smuggler* by Brother Andrew.

Reading aloud can be awkward at first, but after a few minutes, everyone will get into it. You'll be amazed at how expressively your children will read. If you have children too small to read, let them sit in your lap and turn pages.

For a twist, skim a chapter ahead of time and assign sound effects to other members of the family. For example, say, "When you hear the word 'airplane,' make a buzzing noise."

All the News That's Fit to Pray

Do you shake your head as you drink your morning coffee and read the newspaper? Do you feel helpless? The God of Wonders can change things. Tonight, grab the newspaper or a news magazine and parcel it out to your family. (You might want to skim it for objectionable material before you do so.) Have each person read his section. Encourage those too young to read to look very closely at the pictures.

After everyone's had time to read, go around the room and talk about each section. The little ones can talk about the pictures. Be sure to listen well without interrupting—your kid's perspective may teach you something. After everyone has spoken, go back around the room and ask God in prayer for His will to be done in the stories you discussed.

Track one or more of the stories over the coming days and weeks to see what happens.

What Makes Your Garden Grow?

Could your yard use a splash of color? Tonight, plant some flowers and teach a lesson.

Read Mark 4:1-9 to your family. Let your family know that you're going to make this parable come alive in your yard. Set a small spending limit and then go to a nursery. Let your children pick out seeds. You might suggest marigolds or daisies (they are hardy) or recruit the help of a sales clerk.

Once home, have your children throw some seeds on the street or your driveway. Ask them, "What will happen to these seeds?" Then, ask them to gather some rocks from the yard. (Don't have any? Get some pea gravel from a playground at church or school.) Pour some seeds over the rocks. "What do you think will happen to these?"

Lastly, plant some in fertile soil in your yard. Water them and then ask, "What do you think will happen to these?" Watch all three places over the next few days. When the flowers get tall enough, bring some inside and place them in a vase on your family's dinner table.

(Do you live in an apartment? Use three small planters with three types of "soil" in them.)

Our Own ideas

Scripture Journeys

Bible Charades

While this is probably self-explanatory, some pointers might be helpful.

• Stay away from stories or passages that contain strange names.

• Parables, famous Old Testament stories, and scenes from the Acts of the Apostles work best.

• Try to only use one or two verses at a time.

• You may want to go through the Bible and pick several stories in advance. Write each verse (or the gist of the story) on a slip of paper. Put all of the slips in a bowl to be chosen during the game.

The Most Life-Changing Family Endeavor Ever

Joe White, president of Kanakuk Kamps, believes this activity is the most powerful thing his family ever did: his family memorized the entire book of Philippians. If you aren't used to memorizing, it can be hard. It can also be intimidating—your children will learn faster than you!

Don't set your family up for failure! Choose a shorter book like Philemon, 3 John, or Jude. Or you could choose one chapter like Romans 8, Philippians 3, or Psalm 139.

It doesn't have to be a dry experience, either. Push each other. Have a contest with prizes. Say it loudly. Whisper it. March around the house. Make up a song. Listen to a Bible-on-tape and recite along.

Make it fun and discover the riches buried in scripture at the same time.

Bible Trivia

You've probably seen all of the products available. There are games similar to Trivial Pursuit, flash cards, and even computer games. They are all very helpful … and fun. Any one will work well.

My favorite recent addition to the Bible trivia world is a book called *My Final Answer* by Paul Kent. It's set up like (you guessed it) "Who Wants to Be a Millionaire?" It's available from your local Christian retailer or online at any number of book providers, including www.familylife.com

Let the Bible Make You Say WoW!

In 1999, pastors Jeff Schulte and Lloyd Shadrach worked with theologian Carl Laney to develop a Bible reading program that was accessible for families. These three men outlined the plot line of the Bible and divided up the story into seven-minute portions. Each entry leaves you with a cliffhanger—a desire to keep reading to get the rest of the story.

Unfortunately, the book is out of print. But (cue the cheesy television announcer music) have I got a deal for you! The devotional is available free from crosswalk.com. Visit their website at http://devotionals.crosswalk.com. Click on "WoW—the Big Picture" to print out each day's devotional.

Your children will probably ask you to keep reading! Who knows? This might become a nightly habit.

Sword Drills

When I was in fifth grade, my Sunday school teacher paid me five shiny Susan B. Anthony dollars for memorizing the books of the Bible in order. While I'm a little rusty on the minor prophets now, it was a good challenge.

As a family, memorize the books of the Bible. There are some fun songs that can help:

• "The Amazing Book," by Frank and Betsy Hernandez (Bridgestone Video)

• "He Is" by Aaron Jeoffrey (Chordant).

If your children are visual learners, there are some charts and posters that can help as well (ask at your local bookstore).

Once you've memorized the books, have sword drills. If the Bible is the sword of the spirit (Ephesians 6) and is sharper than any two-edged sword (Hebrews 4:12), we need to learn how to use it!

Here's how a sword drill works:

1. Everyone sits with a closed Bible in his or her lap.
2. The judge calls out a Bible passage like "Exodus 20:12."
3. All players scramble through the pages to find the verse.
4. The first person to stand and read the verse wins.

(Team up your pre-readers with older children or have a separate contest where they tell you if the verse is in the Old Testament or New Testament.)

Our own ideas

Focus on Others

Keep America Beautiful

You've seen the signs along the interstate that say, "The next mile adopted by Jim's Weed Wackers. Keep America Beautiful!"

Adopt your own area to keep clean near where you live. Does your neighborhood have an entrance and sign littered by beer cans? Does your apartment complex have a playground with discarded Happy Meal boxes? Does your church have a green space that needs help? Does your school's street appearance leave something to be desired? Pick one area as a family to be your weekly project.

What Does Your Church Need?

The leadership of your church needs help. Tucked among the public jobs of sermon preparation, weddings, funerals, and Vacation Bible School are the hidden tasks:

• Visiting hospital patients
• Helping members move
• Preparing meals for the sick
• Visiting those who can't come on Sundays
• And more

If you attend a small church, the needs are desperate. Even if you attend a large church, there are still things that can be done to lighten the load. What can you do to help? Call the church secretary or someone you know on staff and ask.

Baby-sit for Your Pastor

Pastors face thousands of demands each week. A lot of them meet these time demands by sacrificing some of the time they'd spend with their wives or their children. If your pastor has young children, give him a night off by offering to baby-sit ... for free.

Offer to go over to his house so the kids can go to sleep in their own beds. Bring or fix dinner for the kids. Bring crafts or games. After the kids are asleep, do some dishes or help out in some other way.

Operation Christmas Child

Have you bought school supplies yet for the next school year? Even if you have, go buy some more and send them to the other side of the world. Samaritan's Purse, a ministry headed by Franklin Graham, takes school supplies and health products to children all around the world.

To discover how it works, go to www.samaritanspurse.org. Click on "Operation Christmas Child." You'll find instructions and a list of supplies for your family's box.

My wife cries when we make up shoeboxes. Just thinking about children who don't have a toothbrush or a pencil causes us to thank God for all He's provided for us.

Don't forget to pray for the children who will receive your boxes!

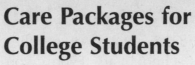

Care Packages for College Students

As exciting as college is, sometimes the stress, loneliness, or homesickness can get the best of even the most well-adjusted student. You probably know a couple of college students. Maybe it's the son of a neighbor. Maybe it's your kids' former babysitter. Perk up her day (or finals week) with a care package from her hometown.

Remind her that she has a family and friends who love her. Pack a box full of things like snack foods, pizza gift certificates, washing detergent, batteries, etc. Don't forget to think about the student's interests. Does she play guitar? Include some picks or maybe a set of strings. Does she love computers? Throw in some blank disks or maybe a new mouse pad. You get the idea. Make it personal and unique.

Most importantly, demonstrate your love by picking some passages of scripture to pray for her. Have each member of the family write a verse on a 3"x5" card and sign it. Include a letter in the box that lets the student know your family will be praying these passages for her. Psalms and the prayers of Paul work really well. Of course, if it's finals week, the entire book of Job might feel more appropriate!

Our own ideas

Home Improvement

Photo Albums

If you're like us, you have several rolls of undeveloped film laying around your house. Even if you're a Creative Memories *aficionado*, you probably feel behind. Get some of the film developed, sit around the kitchen table tonight, and tuck them into a scrapbook. Write captions. Share memories—and laughs—with each other about when and where the pictures were made. Trust me, years from now, you'll appreciate this.

This might also be a good time to catalog your home videotapes. Pop one in and watch as a family. (Go ahead. Make popcorn.) Reset the timer at the beginning of the tape. Every time the scene changes, write down the time and a note to help you find that event later.

Procrastination

What one project around the house have you been postponing? Painting a room? Wallpapering the kitchen? Fixing that leaky sink? Don't put it off anymore. Tonight, get the family together and fix it. Put everybody in the car to go buy supplies. When you get home, give everybody a part of the job and fix it—together. Don't waste a teaching opportunity, either. Go slowly enough to point out what's wrong and how to repair it.

Are you mechanically challenged like me? Ask for help! Surely you have a friend or neighbor who can point you in the right direction. No fear! Just do it!

Car Wash

Have you taught your children how to properly vacuum, wash, and wax a car by hand? Do you even know how yourself? Have fun, get wet, and teach this important lesson. Here are some helpful tips, just in case you need a refresher.

1. Empty trash. Grab an empty bag and fill it with any straw wrappers or petrified french fries that are living under the seats. Tie up and toss it.

2. Wash windows. Spray the insides with glass cleaner. Wipe with lint-free cloth.

3. Vacuum. Get under those floor mats, too!

4. Treat tires. Spray with a tire cleaner. Scrub whitewalls, wheelwells and hubcaps. This is hard work, so rinse before it dries.

5. Lather and rinse the roof.

6. Lather and rinse the rest of car. Pay attention to trouble spots.

7. Dry with a chamois cloth or cotton towels. Don't get tire black on Mom's good bath towels, or you'll be washing the laundry next!

8. Wax on, wax off. Small circles, please, Daniel-san.

9. Spray and wipe exterior windows. Protect the interior. If you opt to use an interior hard surface protectant like Armor-All, stand outside the vehicle and spray it onto a rag to apply. Otherwise you might over-spray and need to re-clean those sparkling windows. Not fun.

Owner for a Day

What would your children do to your home if they owned it (or paid the mortgage or rent)? Make your children "kings/queens for the day" and let them set the agenda. They probably have good ideas and see things you haven't. Obviously some rules are in order.

- Ask good questions and find out what they want to do to the house and yard. Some ideas may be oppressively expensive or too time-intensive, but listen and write down their ideas. You never know, they may have good ones.
- Set a spending limit (even if it's $0).
- Set a time limit (For example: eight work hours).
- Allow them to pick two things that can be done to the house.
- Give options. For instance, if your son says, I don't like the color of my room. I want to paint it bright red," don't slam the door! Acknowledge that he wants to change the color and then work toward a solution.
- Let them feel ownership in the work that needs to be done.

Landmark

I'm one of those people who likes to read the historical markers on vacation. I don't pull the car over for every one, but I enjoy reading the ones we find along the way. Make your home a part of history ... your history.

• Pour some concrete next to your driveway or sidewalk and let everyone make handprints or footprints in it.

• Carve your initials in a tree in the yard.

• Plant a tree (don't forget a brass plaque to commemorate the occasion).

• Buy a new door knocker and have it engraved with your surname and the year you were married. (For example: Whitlock Family/Established 1990)

• Take a family portrait with your house/apartment visible in the background. Frame the picture, caption it, and hang it in a prominent place in your home.

Our Own ideas

You've Got Rhythm

Learn to Waltz

Fred Astaire has nothing on you! Tonight, grab your honey and your kids and cut a rug. Put on anything from "The Tennessee Waltz" to Tchaikovsky's "Waltz of the Flowers" from "The Nutcracker Suite." (You'll instantly recognize it.) From there, it's a simple box step with three beats at every point with a little turn. So what if you don't get it right! You'll have a blast and laugh tons. Don't forget to ask politely for a dance. And last but not least, a waltz wouldn't be complete without a courtly bow.

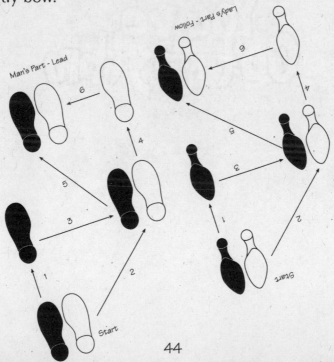

Host a Family Recital

Surely everyone in your family has played an instrument, danced a step, performed a magic trick, sung a tune, or recited a poem at one time or another. Plan a night very soon to gather the entire family together for a recital. Everyone must perform. Costumes are optional—but if your family is like ours, they will be preferred. Once everyone has made a selection, ask the children to make programs and tickets from construction paper. Encourage everyone to practice. When the big night comes, videotape it. If you're adventurous, invite friends and neighbors to watch or even participate.

This is a great motivation for your children to practice. If you have someone in your family who just doesn't fit the "talent show" mold, ask him to be the master of ceremonies or run the video camera. Everyone can take part (and everyone can have his name on the program).

Silly Song Night

Do you remember all those crazy songs you learned growing up like "John Jacob Jingleheimer Schmidt" or "Row, Row, Row Your Boat"? Gather the family together and spend some time singing and making the motions to these wacky numbers. If you're at a loss for titles or tunes, grab a VeggieTales® sing-along video (complete with lyrics on the screen) and sing along!

Listening Party

When record companies release a new recording project, they invite influential people from the music, radio, and journalism industries to have a listen and review the work. They try to create buzz and energy.

Host your own listening party. Prepare some hors d'eouvres. Then, let each person in your family pick out two tracks from his favorite CD. Before each track, have the presenter tell why he likes this song. After each track, go around the room and talk about the strengths of the piece.

You can modify this idea to introduce your family to classical music, jazz, or the "really old songs" you grew up listening to.

Tune My Heart to Sing

If my memory serves me correctly, John Wesley paid his children a shilling for every hymn they learned. In many of our churches, the great hymns of the faith are being replaced by praise choruses. No matter what your worship style preference is, the depth and theology of the hymns is worth learning.

Offer your children a dime for each verse they memorize. Consider these timeless hymns:

- "Holy, Holy, Holy"
- "Crown Him With Many Crowns"
- "Joyful, Joyful, We Adore Thee"
- "Amazing Grace"
- "Christ the Lord Is Risen Today"
- "And Can It Be"
- "When I Survey the Wondrous Cross"
- "O Sacred Head Now Wounded"
- "It Is Well With My Soul"
- "How Great Thou Art"
- "This Is My Father's World"

What are your favorites? Add them to the list. After everyone has learned a few, gather together and sing hymns together. It will be a precious time of worship you'll never forget.

Our Own Ideas

Let The Games Begin

Are You Board?

You've probably seen the commercials that applaud the virtues of a weekly board game night. Tonight, bring the idea home.

We recommend finding a game that will spur conversation and laughter, not silent plotting and strategizing. Have you ever played Life®? While it presents a materialistic worldview, a game can lead to some interesting discussions. The Ungame® is always a discussion starter. Larry Burkett's Money Matters™ is a hit in our home as well as Outburst®. A dear friend of ours plays Masterpiece® about once a week. What's your favorite game? Dust it off and play as a family. Go slowly. Teach your children the rules. We find that in the early stages of learning a game, teams build enthusiasm and understanding.

Famous Active Games

When I was a Boy Scout, we loved to go to the Bixler cabin. My best friend's family owned several acres on a ridge in the Appalachian Mountains. A stream ran under the house.

Our troop would divide up teams for Capture the Flag. The team that lost the coin toss had to hide its flag in the downhill position. We got very serious about the game, including camouflage clothing, face paint, and maps!

When was the last time you played Capture the Flag, Hide and Seek, or Flashlight Tag? These action games are a blast, easy to play, and free! Try one tonight.

Water World

August in Arkansas means temperatures over 100°. The heat and humidity combined can make it feel like it's over 110°! When it's this hot, it's hard—and sometimes dangerous—for children to play outside.

Do you belong to a pool? Do you go often enough to warrant the fee? If not, start now and get your money's worth.

As much as our children love the pool, I think they like to play in the sprinklers or have a water gun battle more. Get creative—and wet—with your family.

Bowling

You may think of bowling alleys as dirty, smoky, and maybe a little dangerous. But have you been to one lately? Many alleys have cleaned up, posted "no smoking" signs, and added computerized scoring.

If this is your child's first time, call ahead and plan your game during a time when the lanes are less busy. Ask the clerk to put gutter covers on a lane for you. This means your children won't have any gutter balls and can have a lot more fun and learn to play more quickly.

If you have older children or experienced bowlers in your family, add a wrinkle. Play one round with your opposite hand (right handed bowlers roll with left hands and vice versa). Play another where you have to approach the lane walking backwards. Play a third where you have to roll the ball between your legs.

Bowling is a great chance for slapping high fives, blowing kisses, and yelling encouraging words while playing. It's also a chance to eat some greasy bowling alley food!

Mad Libs

The other night, during a restaurant visit, my children discovered a mad lib in the children's menu. I'd forgotten how much fun these wacky tales of nonsense can be. A mad lib is a short story with some words missing. The storyteller keeps the story a secret, but goes around the room and asks each person for a word that meets the needs of the story. For instance, some of the words missing may be adjectives, nouns, fruits, names, or animals.

Once the storyteller fills in the blanks, he then reads the story to everyone (if the storyteller can keep from shooting milk out his nose!).

There are books available at general market bookstores or you can write your own. To get you started, we've provided a mad lib below.

Beauty and the Beast Retold

Once upon a _____, a father named _____
(measurement of time)   (middle name of

_____ and his daughter _____ moved to a small
someone in the room)   (family pet's name)

village in _____.
(country in Europe)

One day, the father planned a journey to sell _____.
(kitchen appliance + s)

He _____ a wagon to his _____ and headed to the
         (past-tense verb)   (type of car)

mountains of _____ . After following the _____ road for
              (type of flower)   (type of candy)

miles, he discovered that he was lost. He traipsed a few

hundred yards further, where he stumbled into a small valley.

Tucked on the northern hillside was a magnificent castle, so he

marched up and knocked on its door, hoping to ask for _____
                                                      (something

_____ . The door creaked open, and a burly guardsman
you need on a trip)

snatched _____ by the lapels and tossed him into the
          (middle name from above)

dungeon, where he was forced to eat _____ and _____ .
                                        (sport)   (toy)

     When _____ didn't come home for dinner,
            (middle name from above)

_____ went out to look for him. She followed the
(family pet's name from above)

tracks of the _____ to the castle door. This time, an ugly
               (car from above)

beast answered the knock. He looked like a cross between a

_____ and _____ and his breath smelled like rotten
(animal)   (movie star)

_____ .
(type of cheese)

_____ said to the creature, "Sir, my father is _____
(Family pet's name from above)   (adjective)

and _____. Please don't let him die. Take me instead."
     (adjective)

The beast glared down at her with eyes like those of

aliens from planet _____. "Fine," he growled. He grabbed
                    (favorite store)

her wrist, pitched her in the dungeon, and released her father.

He sent the father home in a _____ truck and ordered
                              (favorite dessert)

him to whistle the theme from _____ all the way home.
                                (TV show)

Back at the castle, _____ peered through the
                    (pet's name from above)

barred window of the dungeon and shouted, "You don't have

to be a beast! You could be like _____ instead. All you
                                 (favorite teacher)

have to do is _____and brush your_____. Then your warts
              (name a chore)   (body part)

will fall off and you can be normal again."

The beast, who was crawling up the stairs from the dank cellar, turned back in surprise. He growled. He scratched his calloused_____ . "Hmm. I could do that," he said. "How

(body part)

long will it take?"

The girl replied, "Only _____ years."

(favorite number)

The End

Excursions

Say Thank You

During the Persian Gulf War, I realized that I had taken the men and women of our armed forces for granted. Since then, I've made it a point to say "thank you" to all of the service personnel I meet.

Tonight, make a family outing of saying "thank you." Is there a military base nearby? How about a fire station, hospital, or police station? Who else protects and serves you? Give it a little thought. Call ahead and find out where to go and when it's best for visitors to come by. Take some cookies or banana bread along as a tangible "thank you" or make a big card out of poster board.

Local Tourist

I grew up in Stone Mountain, Ga. Even though I went to Stone Mountain Park once a week for the laser show or a jog, I never visited the Antique Car Museum. Just last summer, after being gone 14 years, I finally took the tour.

If a friend or relative were coming in from out of town, where would you tell him to visit? Have you visited there yourself? Make a point very soon to take your family to visit this tourist attraction in your own backyard. Be real tourists—take pictures and buy cheap souvenirs.

Behind the Scenes

Have you ever wondered what it takes to make a pizza, deliver milk to the grocery store, or get an airplane ready to fly? Many businesses offer "behind the scenes" tours that can give your family more appreciation for what goes into the goods and services you use as a family. A call to the manager of a restaurant or the public relations department of a large company is all that's needed to set up a tour.

Sure, not every establishment offers this service. If you strike out on some of the more adventurous outings, McDonald's and Domino's Pizza are always fun and exciting.

Fun places to go "behind the scenes":

Movie theater projection room
Bakery
Post office
Dairy
Concert hall
Car dealership
Factory
Donut shop
Restaurant
Radio or TV station
Advertising company
Print shop
Newspaper or magazine

Blindfold Discovery

Everyday, we are bombarded with thousands of visual images. The onslaught of advertising causes us to rely on our sense of sight—while we ignore our other four senses. Tonight, blindfold everyone in the family except you and go on an adventure in sound, fragrance, flavor, and texture. Some of you may want to go a local botanical garden or greenhouse. Others may head to the zoo. The shopping mall can be fun, too. For a twist, drive around with everyone blindfolded for a while and then go back to your house. Experience your yard in a new way!

Scavenger Hunt

Everyone loves the idea of hunting for treasure. Give your family an adventure they'll never forget tonight. Create a scavenger hunt for things that begin with each letter of the alphabet or that symbolize the fruits of the spirit (Galatians 5). For an added twist, borrow some instant cameras and have each team take pictures as they solve each clue.

Our Own Ideas

Creative Classics

Paint a Classic

Are there budding artists in your home? Gather the crayons, watercolors, and art paper together in the kitchen. Dress everyone in sloppy smocks and experience art appreciation in a new way. Find one or more classic pieces of art in a book, magazine, or at the library. Show the artwork to your family and tell them the story behind the painting. Then go around the table and let everyone make observations about it. If the conversation stalls, play Twenty Questions or I Spy about the piece of artwork.

After you've dissected the artist's work, ask everyone to copy the painting. This is a great way to teach basic art skills and just have fun.

For a twist or if you're short on examples of classic art, try painting self-portraits.

Paper Airport

We love paper airplanes in our family. The other day, our son and a friend created an airport. They made different kinds of airplanes and created paper "gates" for each type of plane. Create La Guardia or Hartsfield in your home!

There are a number of websites and books on how to make good paper airplanes. Do a search online or get a book from the library or bookstore and have fun tonight.

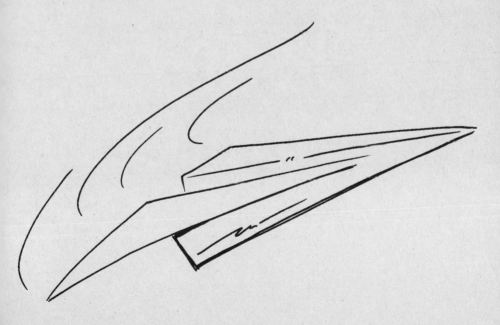

Request Night

After you've hosted family fun nights for a while, you'll discover that your children want to repeat one. Make tonight "request" night. Encourage the kids to decide which activity the family should repeat. Then, just do it!

Family Theater

If Shakespeare is right and "all the world's a stage," turn your home into a center for performing arts. Get together and create a play or a puppet show and present it as a family. Adapt a favorite Bible story or fairy tale for your special evening. Don't forget sets, costumes, and programs. Invite friends, family, or neighbors over to applaud.

If your ideas seem to fall apart, go to your Christian bookstore and look through some of the skit books. There are many good ones—including some skits adapted from the "Adventures in Odyssey" episodes.

Write Your Own Story

Create a storybook that your family can share and enjoy for years to come. Start by choosing one of the story openings below. Then take turns adding a sentence.

My younger daughter, Lauren, loves this story opening:

"Long ago and far away beyond the land of dreams, a princess named ..."

My son, Michael, prefers that he set the tone first, and then I build the plot around the problem that we established in the beginning of the story ....

"There once was a boy named _____. His favorite thing to do was _____. But he didn't get to do his favorite thing very often because _____."

Starting with action is always a good idea. Let the "back story" come out as you tell it. For example, "The gushing water pitched their raft up, then down. Jared and Jenna gripped the nylon rope tightly with both hands. Each took a moment to free a hand and wipe ice-cold river water from their eyes. It was then that they noticed the boulder in their path. In the same moment, they turned to each other and shouted, "Ahhhhh!"

And of course, there's the classic: "Once upon a time ..."

Our Own ideas

Literature Library

Book of Poetry

Most of us take poetry for granted. Or maybe it's that we're intimidated by those who write it well. Regardless of your apprehensions, pluck a book of poetry from a bookstore shelf and plunk down your money. You may find that your kids enjoy it. For young ones, I recommend Shel Silverstein or Dr. Seuss. Your older children might enjoy Walt Whitman or Robert Frost.

Read a Great Fantasy

Harry Potter[3] has been a fascination for the last three years. The hype will only build through the release of more books and more motion pictures. No matter where you stand on the "Harry issue," fantasy literature is making a comeback. Many of these novels make great reading for families. Some, like *The Chronicles of Narnia* by C. S. Lewis, can edify your family and spark great spiritual discussions.

[3] To read FamilyLife's statement on Harry Potter, go to www.familylife.com. In the left-hand navigation bar, you'll find a search window. Type in Harry Potter. Many entries will come up. Under the articles section, you'll find "Who is J. K. Rowling?" and other articles.

The Theater of the Mind

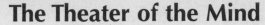

Before the advent of television, families used to gather around the console radio and tune in to far-away New York City. Through the static, they would hear dramas like "The Green Hornet" or "The Shadow." During this golden age of audio drama, Hiram Brown, the producer of CBS Mystery Theatre, called radio the "theater of the mind."

Stimulate the imaginations of your family by gathering around your hi-fi stereo rack system. Listen to a great audio book or audio drama. I'd encourage you to break up your listening into several nights to keep suspense high.

Suggestions:

• Focus on the Family's "Adventures in Odyssey" are always good. If you're new to Odyssey, I'd recommend starting with a series like "Daring Deeds, Sinister Schemes" or "The Early Classics." If you're a fan, revisit multi-part adventures like "The Passover" or "The Mortal Coil."

• Focus on the Family Radio Theatre has also produced many great classics including "The Chronicles of Narnia" and "Les Miserables." If you have older children, start with "Bonnhoeffer: The Cost of Freedom."

• Excellent audio books included "The Hiding Place," Bodie Thoene's Zion Covenant series, "This Present Darkness," and "Left Behind."

CAUTION: **Don't let this become a substitute for television!**

Family Journal

One summer, we encouraged our children to keep their writing skills sharp and chronicle our summer adventures in journals. We used three-ring binders with pockets on the outside. Each child created a cover for his or her journal. We then filled them with standard-rule notebook paper. We asked our children to write at least five sentences a day. We missed more days than we wrote, but it was a great process. I know these will be treasured keepsakes someday.

All the Couch Is a Stage

How many of you actually like Shakespeare? I know quotes that can be attributed to Shakespeare but I have no idea to what play. As a family, why don't you dip your thespian toes into the waters of the most influential writer in the English language? Grab a copy of a play like *Romeo and Juliet* or *A Midsummer Night's Dream* and read parts as a family. A copy of Cliff's Notes for the play or an online synopsis can help a great deal to orient you to what is intended. Don't be afraid of the man from Stratford-upon-Avon or his writing. Who knows, you might like the footlights.

Our own ideas

Family Ties

Homemade Hand Crank Ice cream

If your shoulder has never ached from cranking an ice cream maker, then you haven't lived. But it's not the pain that makes this activity worthwhile, it's the ice cream. Choose a recipe for your favorite flavor, buy the ingredients, and get ready to beef up your biceps!

If you have the electric-style ice cream maker, bring a bit of nostalgia to the chore by inviting grandparents or an elderly neighbor. Ask them to share their stories of making ice cream in the days before Frigidaire.

Name Acronyms

We recently featured two guests on "FamilyLife Today" who helped us with practical suggestions for stopping whining in our homes.[4] One of the keys suggested by Scott Turansky and Joanne Miller is

"honor." You can have your family display honor with this easy exercise:

- Give each member of the family several sheets of paper.
- Make sure everyone has a pen.
- Write the first name of each family member in a vertical line on a separate sheet of paper.
- Think through words that begin with each letter that describe that person.

When everyone is finished, pick someone out of the family to sit in a special chair. Then go around and let each member of the family read his or her acronym. After everyone has had a turn, close in prayer, thanking God for your special family.

As an example, here's what our older daughter wrote about her brother:

Monster
Intelligent
Caring
Hugger
Active
Energetic
Laughter

[4] If you'd like to listen to this material, go to www.familylife.com. Search our site for "say goodbye to whining."

Postcard Extravaganza

The year after e-mail became a national craze, stock in companies like Mont Blanc, Shaeffer, and Cross became hot commodities. Why? Because a fine writing instrument became a status symbol. In the same way, business communication books and articles now celebrate the importance of a handwritten note to staff members and co-workers. They say the value is unsurpassed.

If a handwritten note means so much, make the best of it. Go to the local discount store and buy a ton of postcards. Gather around the table with your address book and have everyone write to aunts, uncles, cousins, grandparents, friends, missionaries, old teachers, college roommates, or coaches.

Don't forget the stamps!

Photo Album Night

Every New Year's Eve, the Rainey family gathers around a bonfire and reminisces about the previous year while looking through the photo album. It's a family tradition that will never be forgotten.

When was the last time you looked through your photo albums? Tonight, gather the family together and tell all the old stories about your wedding day, your honeymoon, when children were born or adopted, Christmases past, and favorite vacations.

Reach Out and Hug Someone

In the 1980s, the phone companies had the best advertising agencies. Before the dime wars began, long distance companies showed the phone calls that made you cry. Experience one of those yourself by calling a friend or family member you haven't talked to in a long time.

Before you call, ask each person in the family to think about a story or interesting fact of life he or she would like to share. Place the call and enjoy!

If you're worried about your phone bill, buy a pre-paid phone card from a discount store. That way, you know how much you're going to spend and you won't be surprised when Ma Bell contacts you again.

Now It's Your Turn!

What else does your family do to build relationships, connect with each other, and have fun? Throughout this book, we've provided a number of pages for you to record your ideas for the months and years to come. You can also use them to write down your memories of your TV fast.

Let us know your ideas.

Go to www.familylife.com/familyfun/ and send us an e-mail. We'd love to hear your ideas!

You can also write to us at:

Fifty Nights of Family Fun
c/o FamilyLife
5800 Ranch Drive
Little Rock, AR 72223

Our own ideas

Author Bio

Mark Whitlock has spent more than a decade helping families grow stronger and closer together. Mark worked for Focus on the Family before joining the staff of FamilyLife, where he has served as an engineer/producer for the daily radio program "FamilyLife Today." Mark has been responsible for and has contributed as an author to FamilyLife resources like Passport to Purity, Simply Romantic Nights, and A Very Veggie Family Adventure. He lives and laughs with his wife and their three children in Little Rock, Ark.